JUNGLE TRAIL

Written by Fiona Waters

Illustrated by Gary Boller

HENDERSON
PUBLISHING LTD

©1997 HENDERSON PUBLISHING LTD

What is a Rain Forest?

About a third of the Earth's land is covered in forests. The largest forest of all is called the Taiga and it runs across Canada, Scandinavia and the Russian Federation. It is always bitterly cold there and, for several months of the year, dark all the time. The tropical rain forests are very different.

Rain forests are always hot, about 27-28°C (80-82°F), and it rains every day. The warm, damp *environment* is very good for plants and animals, and the forests are home to about half the world's plant and animal *species*.

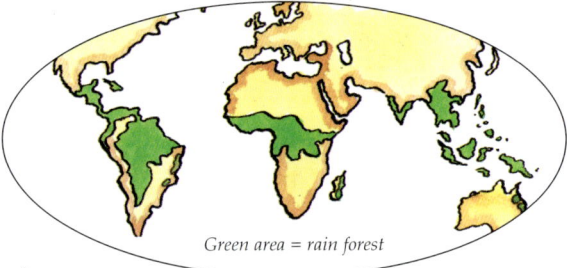

Green area = rain forest

Ant-astic

The largest rain forest is around the Amazon River in South America. It covers an area of 7 million sq km (2.7 million sq miles). A single tree in the Amazon basin can be home to as many as 43 different species of ant!

Amazon rain forest

Going Down

A rain forest consists of several layers of *vegetation* (plant life). At the very top is the *emergent* layer formed by the tops of the very highest trees.

Emergent layer

Next down is the *canopy* layer. Most of the animals and birds live here as there is plenty of food, water and light.

Canopy

Below the canopy is the *understory* where climbing plants twine themselves around the tree trunks.

Understory

Forest floor

Finally, at the bottom there is the *forest floor*. Not much grows here apart from *fungi* and *parasites*, and plants wherever the light manages to get through.

JUNGLE TRAIL 3

From the Top...

In some rain forests there is a layer even higher than the emergent layer called the *cloud forest*. This area is shrouded in heavy mist and is cool and very damp, so all the trees are covered in mosses and seaweed-like plants called liverworts.

Liverwort

The Top Floor
In most rain forests, the emergent layer trees are far taller than any of the others, rising to as high as 60-70 m (200-230 ft) above the ground. The tallest broad-leaved rain forest tree recorded is a tualang at 87 m (285 ft) tall.

Roof-top Inhabitants
The black and white colobus monkey lives up in the tree tops where it feeds on the leaves. It has to be very wary of one of its neighbours, the harpy eagle. One of the world's largest eagles, this bird is quite happy to have a sloth or a monkey for supper! Delicious!

Colobus monkey

LEAFY CANOPY

At the canopy level, 25-45 m (82-148ft) above the forest floor, it is leafy all the year round. Some trees may shed their leaves, but only for a few days. Most of the leaves have a shiny surface so that the rainwater slides off quickly to prevent the growth of *algae,* a type of plant. Ingenious!

Typical rain forest leaf

TARZAN'S ROPES

At canopy level, there are many plants that need light to survive, so they use the tall rain forest trees as supports to climb up. They are called *lianas,* and they can grow amazingly quickly, forming natural ropes. The fictional character Tarzan used lianas to swing from tree to tree across the jungle!

HIDDEN LIFE

The canopy is teeming with life. Birds, butterflies, animals, insects, flowers and plants are in super abundance here. Many are never seen on the forest floor and it wasn't until biologists erected walkways high up in the trees that many species became known.

White-lipped tree frog

... To the Bottom

The forest floor is very shady and the air is almost completely still. Only about two per cent of the light reaches it through the canopy. The ground is carpeted with roots and twigs, and only when a tree falls down, letting more light through, do other plants shoot up. Extra light can make giant bamboos put on a huge spurt of growth – up to 23 cm (9 in) a day!

Mushrooms on Toast?
Fungi grow very quickly in the *humidity* (dampness) of the forest floor. They take *nutrients* (mineral nourishment) from the dead leaves and are often very brightly coloured, and highly poisonous.

Deep-rooted
Because rain forest trees have to grow to such huge heights to find light, they are in danger of toppling over. They avoid this by producing *buttress roots* which spread out to an enormous size. They sometimes spread up the tree to a height of 9 m (30 ft).

WET UNDERFOOT

With all the rain that it gets, the rain forest is running with water which eventually drains into the rivers. When rain forest rivers flood, *swamp forests* are created where the *silt* (a muddy deposit) covers the surrounding land. Where the rivers go into the sea, *mangrove swamps* are formed. These swamplands are home to many thousands of fish, snakes and plants.

DANGER!

There are dangers lurking in the rain forest. Piranha fish are found in rain forest waters. With their rows of sharp, triangular teeth they are to be avoided. When water levels are low in the dry season, they gather in shoals of 20 or more and are able to attack quite large prey.

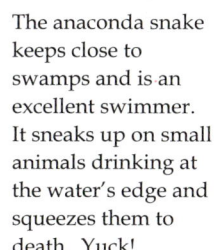

Piranha fish

The anaconda snake keeps close to swamps and is an excellent swimmer. It sneaks up on small animals drinking at the water's edge and squeezes them to death. Yuck!

Anaconda

CENTRAL AMERICAN JUNGLES

The narrow neck of land called an *isthmus,* that joins North and South America, was once the centre of two amazing civilizations – the Mayans and the Aztecs. They left behind many examples of pottery showing the rich variety of animals to be found there.

DISAPPEARING RAIN FOREST
Almost all the Caribbean islands were covered with rain forests at one time, but they have gradually been cleared to make way for sugar *plantations.* Sugar cane is one of the major crops in Central America.

NOISY TREE-DWELLERS
Macaws are vividly-coloured, noisy birds which live high up in the trees, with their nests often over 30 m (98 ft) above the ground. They are expert fliers with short, broad wings and can actually brake before landing on a tree or branch. They live on seeds which they crack open with their pincer-like beaks.

Golden Beetle

The jewel-like golden beetle is about 3 cm (over 1 in) long and lives only in Costa Rica. The adults chomp their way through leaves, while the young, called *larvae,* feed on soft rotting plants.

Golden beetle

Small is Beautiful

Although the countries in Central America are small, they are amazingly rich in resources. They export many tropical crops such as avocado pears, pawpaws, vanilla and allspice.

Believe It or Not...

The tiny Central American republic of Panama has more birds than the whole of North America.

JUNGLE TRAIL

SOUTH AMERICAN JUNGLE

South America is a place of extremes. Here are some of its main features:

- The world's longest mountain chain, the Andes, dominates South America and is 7,200 km (4,500 miles) long.
- The Amazon River is 6,439 km (4,001 miles) long.
- The Atacama Desert in Chile is the world's driest place.
- Over 11,700 mm (460 in) of rain falls in parts of Colombia. Don't forget your umbrella!

Believe It or Not...

About 180,000 cu m (6.4 million cu ft) of water pours out of the Amazon River into the Atlantic Ocean every second. The river could fill St Paul's Cathedral in London in just over a second. Phew!

Big, Bigger and Best

The Amazonian rain forest is home to about one fifth of the world's bird and flowering plant species, and about one tenth of the world's mammal species. The three-toed sloth (on the left) lives here, doing very little apart from hanging upside-down!

Golden Monkey
The golden tamarin monkey can only be found in Atlantic coastal rain forests. Tamarins were recently close to *extinction* (dying out) as they were exported as pets, and too much of their natural habitat was being destroyed.

Golden tamarin

Lip Gloss
One of the ingredients in lipstick is often *carnauba wax* which comes from the Brazilian wax palm. Young leaves are picked and dried in the sun until the wax flakes off. About 1,300 leaves are needed to get only 1 kg (2.2 lb) of wax.

Wax palm

Special Brew
The Amazon lily is believed to have mysterious powers. Tribes in Colombia and Ecuador boil the whole plant, including the bulb, to make a tea that the men drink before they go hunting.

JUNGLE TRAIL

EXOTIC SPECIMENS

Next time you consider going on a trek through the rain forest, make a note to look out for the exotic specimens shown on these pages.

LEAFY CANAL
When the leaves of water lilies first emerge they are rolled up in tubes underwater. In the spring, the leaves come to the surface and open out to lie flat. The leaves of the Amazonian water lily can reach a diameter of more than 2 m (6 ft) and can support the weight of a young child.

HIGH-RISE ROOTS
Usually, trees cannot grow in waterlogged soil as the ground is too unstable and is very low in *oxygen*, which tree roots need. Mangrove trees have adapted to their watery surroundings by having two kinds of roots. *Stilt roots* come from the tree trunk and put an anchor down in the mud. *Breathing roots*, called *pneumatophores* (on the right), come up out of the water so that they can take in oxygen. Smart, huh?

Float Like a Butterfly

Gorgeously-coloured butterflies are to be found all over the world in tropical rain forests, but the biggest variety live in South America. With no winter and many different plants to feed on, butterflies flourish here. Some look quite spectacular with glowing colours, while others are so well *camouflaged* that they are almost totally hidden.

South American camouflaged butterfly

Swallowtail

Bright Lights

Collecting jungle insects for research is always difficult. They are attracted by *ultraviolet light,* so scientists rig up large bags with a light above them and the insects usually fall for it! Every bag may contain thousands of different species.

African Rain Forests

The African rain forests are in a small part of the central region, along the *equator* and beside the western coast. They have much fewer plant and animal species than other rain forests in the world.

Orchid

Hibiscus

Exotic Flowers
There are around 18,000 species of orchid and many of these are found in rain forests. Over 60 per cent of the plants in the canopy of the African rain forests are orchids, and many of these have not yet been identified.

The hibiscus is another flourishing rain forest flower. It can grow up to 2 m (6 ft) tall.

Home Weaving
The West African weaverbird builds the most extraordinary nest, in a kind of trumpet shape. This design is intended to prevent snakes from getting inside. The bird uses its amazing skill of tying knots with its beak and feet to build its complex home.

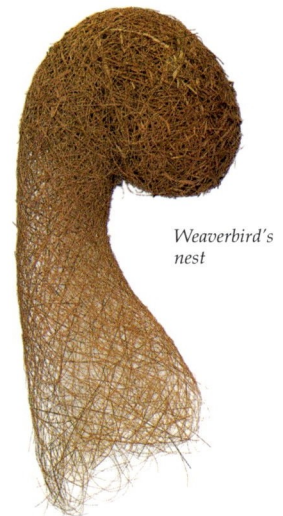

Weaverbird's nest

THE GIANTS
Gorillas and elephants browse slowly through the forest vegetation eating their favourite leaves, stems and fruit. Find out more on pages 20-23 and pages 26-27.

PARROT PERKS
Senegal parrots migrate from the surrounding grasslands to the rain forests for a change of diet! They are very fond of the fruit and seeds to be found in the forest, and make their nests in unlined tree holes.

Senegal parrot

VELCRO FEET
The day gecko from Madagascar has sticky pads on its toes, like velcro, so it can hold tightly on to branches, even when it is upside-down!

ASIAN RAIN FORESTS

The word *jungle* actually comes from the Hindi word *jangal* which means 'impenetrable forest'. The jungle left in India and Southeast Asia has enormously varied animal and plant life. A great amount of the territory is made up of islands and *archipelagos* (groups of islands) – some huge and some tiny.

THREE-PIECE SUITE
One of the most important *exports* (goods sold to a foreign country) from the Asian rain forests is *rattan*. Rattans are climbing palms whose stems can reach enormous heights and are sometimes over 200 m (660 ft) in length. Rattan canes are made into garden and conservatory furniture. There are over 600 species of rattan – that's a lot of chairs!

FLYING FROGS...
Flying frogs can leap from tree to tree to escape their enemies. They have very large webbed 'hands' and 'feet' which act as parachutes when the creatures are airborne. Wheeeeeee!

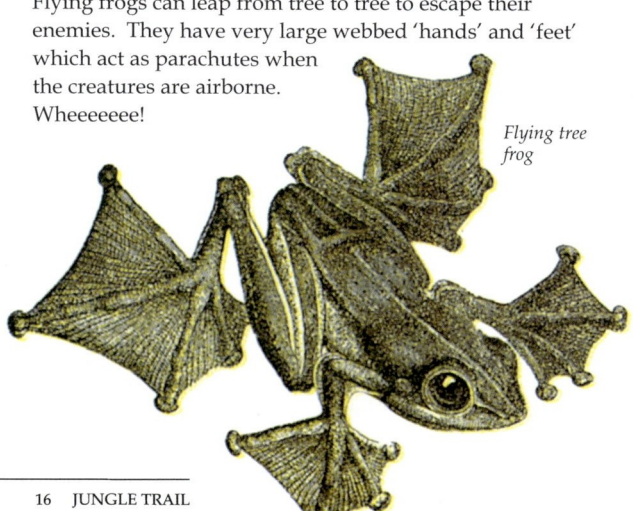

Flying tree frog

...AND FLYING SNAKES!

The flying snake can travel amazing distances through the air! It can leap over 50 m (164 ft) from one tree to another. It raises its ribs upwards and outwards so its body is almost flat, only to resume its normal shape when it lands. Sneaky, huh?

FLOWERY SHOES?

There are about 70 species of tropical slipper orchid, most of which grow on the forest floor in the Asian jungle. They are very rare as they can only grow in very specialized habitats. Most of them grow on the ground, although some grow on rocks or trees.

Tropical slipper orchid

JUNGLE TRAIL 17

AUSTRALASIAN RAIN FORESTS

Millions of years ago, Australia and Antarctica were joined together and the coastal area of this huge *continent* (landmass) was covered with rain forest. Australia then drifted north and became drier, and the present day rain forests are the remains of this ancient jungle. Most of the rain forest lies in New Guinea, to the north of Australia. Many parts are so remote that they have not yet been explored.

CROAK, CROAK!
White's tree frog lives in the forests, but its habit of popping up in water barrels and lavatories means it is well-known to most Australians!

SHOW-OFF
The male bird of paradise has the most spectacular plumage, especially designed to hook a mate! As day breaks and sunlight filters through the leaves, these birds swoop through the trees, flashing their fine feathers and calling loudly.

SHY BEAUTY

One of the world's rarest butterflies, Queen Alexandra's birdwing, lives in a very small part of Papua New Guinea. Little is known about this butterfly other than it is one of the largest. The female, which is bigger than the male, can have a wingspan of up to 28 cm (11 in).

Queen Alexandra's birdwing

CARRIER BAG BABIES

Apart from bats, all the native animals in the Australasian rain forests are *marsupials*. These are animals where the female gives birth to babies which then develop inside her pouch, until they are ready to fend for themselves.

You are probably familiar with kangaroos, but what about the tree kangaroo? These distant relatives of ground kangaroos climb the trees to eat the leaves, yet are still able to hop along the ground.

JUNGLE TRAIL 19

ELEPHANTS – GENTLE GIANTS

Elephants of the present and the past have lived just about everywhere, except Australia and Antarctica. They have roamed deserts, rain forests and even glaciers.

A Mixed Relationship?

Elephants and humans have a very mixed relationship. In some countries elephants are seen as useful workers and ceremonial beasts of burden, but in others they are killed for their ivory tusks.

Jumbo

The African elephant is the largest land animal in the world today. A male elephant, known as a *bull*, can stand 4 m (13 ft) tall and weigh as much as 6,048 kg (13,335 lb). The females, known as *cows*, are smaller.

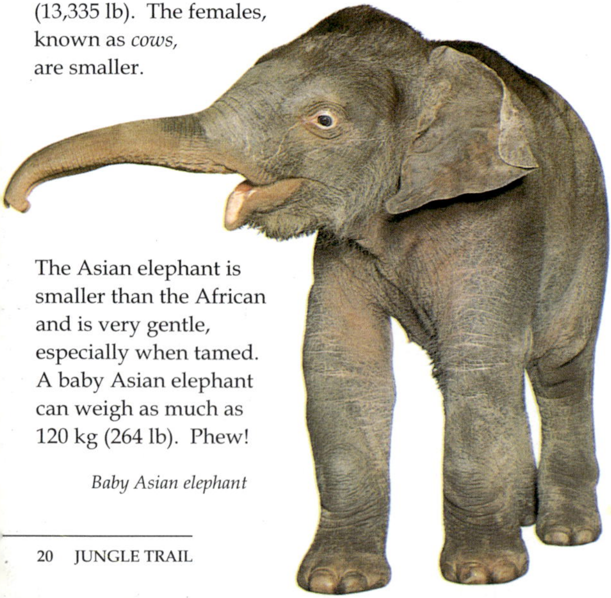

The Asian elephant is smaller than the African and is very gentle, especially when tamed. A baby Asian elephant can weigh as much as 120 kg (264 lb). Phew!

Baby Asian elephant

Dainty Feet

Elephants are surprisingly light on their feet for such big creatures. In fact, they walk on tiptoe. Look at this cross section of an elephant's foot and all will become clear!

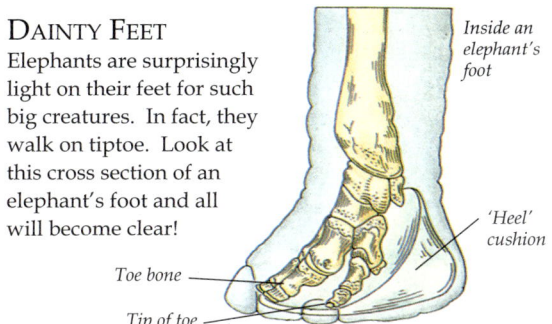

Inside an elephant's foot

'Heel' cushion

Toe bone

Tip of toe

The sole of an elephant's foot looks rather like a dried up river bed with many ridges and cracks. This gives it a good grip when travelling over uneven ground.

Trunk Call

The elephant's trunk is like a nose, an arm and a hand all rolled into one! African elephants even have two 'fingers' at the end of their trunk, enabling them to pick up quite small objects. Such a clever organ gets tired sometimes, so the elephant drapes it across one of its tusks for a rest!

Elephant Life

In elephant society, bulls and cows do not live together. The cows and calves are always in a group led by the *matriarch*, who is usually a grandmother or even a great-grandmother. The bulls spend most of their time alone, or sometimes with a group of other males.

Baby Talk
Baby elephants must sometimes feel that they live in a world of legs, as the cows always group protectively around them. There is always an aunt or a big sister to help the babies out if they get stuck in mud or caught in low-hanging branches.

Bad Boys
The bulls are much more interested in their reputation amongst the other males than in family life. They indulge in great trials of strength to show who is most powerful, but no one ever gets seriously hurt.

Food and Drink
Needless to say, such huge animals have huge appetites! The great mound of food shown here is a typical day's food for an elephant in a zoo.

BELIEVE IT OR NOT...
An adult elephant needs to drink about 225 litres (50 gallons) of water a day.

ALL IN A DAY'S WORK
Some of the earliest working elephants crossed the Alps with Hannibal (247-182 BC), the young North African general who stopped the mighty Roman army in its tracks with his animal 'tanks'.

Elephants are still used today in wars in Southeast Asian jungles, as they can move quietly without leaving any tracks, and soldiers on their backs have a good view of the countryside.

Elephants are peacetime workers too. They can pull logs weighing more than 4 tonnes and lift smaller timbers with their trunks.

What is a Primate?

Primates are a varied group of *mammals* (animals which give birth to live young and feed them with their milk). They include monkeys, apes and humans! Most of them live in trees and their bodies are especially made for this lifestyle.

Old World
Old World monkeys live in Asia and Africa and are the largest and most varied group of primates.

The proboscis monkey is an Old World monkey with an enormous drooping nose, which can be as long as 7.6 cm (3 in) in an adult male. It likes to swim, which is unusual for a monkey, and has been known to take a high dive from 15 m (50 ft) into the water!

Proboscis monkey

NEW WORLD

New World monkeys live in the jungles of Central and South America. They are all tree-dwelling and many have *prehensile* tails – that is, a tail that can be used as another arm or leg, for gripping. These monkeys can hang from a branch by the tail only!

Howler monkey – its howls echo around the jungle as it marks its territory

Woolly monkey – very woolly with an extra strong tail

Spider monkey – fruit-eater with a passion for passion fruit!

Capuchin monkey – the most intelligent New World monkey

UPRIGHT SLEEPER

Baboons have *nonprehensile* tails (no good for grasping) and large red *sitting pads* which help them to sleep sitting up. They are *carnivores* (meat-eaters) and sometimes hunt young gazelles (antelopes) in groups.

The Great Apes

The four great apes – the gorilla, chimpanzee, orang-utan and bonobo – are much larger than monkeys and do not have tails. They are very intelligent and share many characteristics with humans.

Gentle Giants

The image many people have of a gorilla is based on the movie *King Kong*. Although an angry male gorilla about to charge is a terrifying sight, he only does this when provoked and if his family is in danger. Gorillas are generally easy-going, gentle creatures who like to sleep, eat and play!

Dinner Time

Gorillas are very fussy about their food and only select choice plants. They eat nettles, thistles and wild celery, with bamboo as a special treat. They usually eat sitting down with their huge tummies resting between their knees.

GORILLA BABIES

Like human babies, baby gorillas are helpless and totally dependent on their mothers. They are very small, only 2-3 kg (4-6 lb), and their fur begins to grow within days of being born. At about six months old they can romp around with other 'toddlers'.

Young gorillas playing

CLOSE RELATIONS

Chimpanzees are the closest apes to humans in appearance and behaviour. They are highly intelligent and can use rocks to crack open nuts, and sticks to poke out delicious insect nests. They spend hours grooming each other's fur.

Chimpanzees live in large communities of up to 80. When friends meet, they hoot and hug each other, but rivals eye each other up and down. The oldest chimpanzees are treated with considerable respect.

Baby chimpanzees

JUNGLE TRAIL

Stranger Still

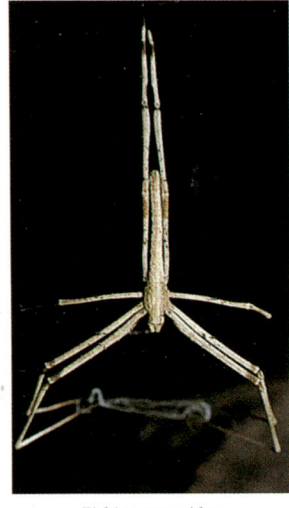

Fishing net spider

There are many strange and wonderful insects, spiders, butterflies, snakes, frogs, bats and other animals to be found in the rain forest.

A Crafty Trap

The fishing net spider doesn't spin a web for insects to blunder into, as other spiders do. It hangs upside-down from a twig and drops the web over its prey! Nifty stuff!

Blooming Marvellous!

The female orchid mantis lurks in the flower head of an orchid looking just like part of the bloom. Down comes an unsuspecting insect and she lashes out with her deadly front legs.

Lurking orchid mantis

All Lit Up
Fireflies are not flies but beetles. Their abdominal organs make light to attract other fireflies, not to see where they are going!

Fruitcase
Fruit bats have huge eyes and very good vision, but they use their noses and sense of smell to locate supper!

Night-time Visitor
The tapir is a little-known solitary creature that comes out at night-time. It uses its long snout to rootle for fruits and seeds among the leaves on the forest floor.

Tapir

Two to Avoid!
The blue poison dart frog lives on the forest floor and gives off very nasty poisons from its skin.

The cobra is a deadly snake which rears up from the ground with a hiss as it puffs out its hood and injects its victim with a very toxic venom from its front fangs.

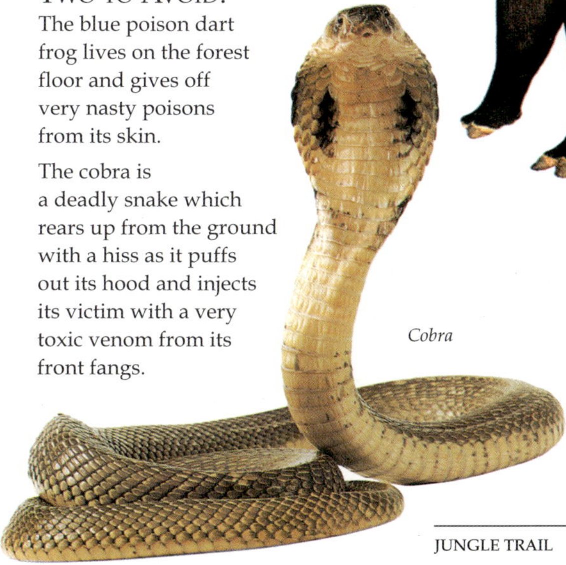

Cobra

JUNGLE TRAIL

The Jungle's Big Cats

Tigers are the most powerful cats of all, and can be found from icy Siberia to tropical India. There are lots of other members of the big cat family around the world. Here are a few to get your teeth into.

The Clouded Leopard
The clouded leopard is a beautiful creature, rarely seen and now in danger of extinction. It lives in the forests of Southeast Asia.

Hidden Spots
The mysterious-looking black panther is just a leopard with its spots hidden! Mowgli, the boy in Rudyard Kipling's *Jungle Book*, was brought up by the black panther Bagheera.

Black panther

AMERICAN BIG CAT

The jaguar is the only big cat to be found in America. Its name comes from the Amazonian word *yaguara*. Its spots help it blend into its forest surroundings. It swims in the rivers of the tropical forest where it has been known to kill crocodiles!

SMALLER KITTIES

There are several smaller wild cats living in forests or jungles on every continent, except Australasia. They are usually solitary hunters and very little is known about them.

Margay – looks like an ocelot (another type of cat) and feeds on birds

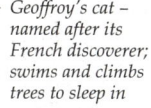

Geoffroy's cat – named after its French discoverer; swims and climbs trees to sleep in

Deadly Danger!

The jungle is full of deadly dangers with both animals and plants kitted out with poisons and killing equipment.

Don't Pick the Flowers!
The passion flower's leaves contain toxic chemicals including *cyanide*, so mammals soon learn to avoid it.

Screw pines are tropical plants whose sword-shaped leaves have vicious barbs along the edges.

Fantastic Flutterer
The enormous African giant swallowtail butterfly can have a wingspan of up to 250 mm (10 in). It is very poisonous and is completely avoided by all its enemies.

African giant swallowtail

Not Too Tight!
The boa constrictor grabs its prey with its mouth and then coils itself around the animal's body. Each time the animal breathes out, the snake tightens its grip until the prey is suffocated.

Boa constrictor dining on a rat

Mind Your Feet

The giant tiger centipede has vivid stripes across its body warning that it is poisonous.

The tarantula injects its prey with a venom that causes almost immediate paralysis.

Tarantula

Water Feature

The crocodile is the largest of the jungle predators and can reach over 6 m (20 ft) in length. It is capable of incredible bursts of speed and grabs its prey with its frighteningly sharp teeth, holding the creature underwater until it drowns.

Nile crocodile

DOCTOR, DOCTOR

The tribal people of the rain forests know an enormous amount about the plants that grow around their homes. They eat many of them and use others as medicines.

QUININE
A disease called *malaria*, caused by mosquito bites, can be treated with quinine. This comes from the bark of the South American cinchona tree.

Quinine stored in bark

THE ORDEAL BEAN
The very poisonous seeds of the calabar bean, or *ordeal beans* as they were known, were used to decide a person's guilt. If they survived eating the beans, they were innocent...and very, very lucky! Extracts from the seeds are now used to treat high blood pressure and an eye disease called *glaucoma*.

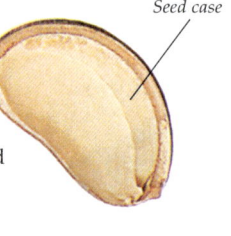

Seed case

Calabar bean

Seed kernel

34 JUNGLE TRAIL

Flowering of Hope

The rosy periwinkle which grows in Africa has helped in the treatment of two kinds of cancer – *Hodgkin's disease* and *leukaemia*.

Rosy periwinkle

Yam, Yam

The yam is eaten as a vegetable, but it also contains chemicals which are used to treat *rheumatic fever* and *rheumatoid arthritis*.

Natural Toothbrushes

For centuries, tribes people in Africa have used chew sticks to keep their teeth clean. In fact, one tree is called the toothbrush tree! The juices released seem to prevent *bacteria* surviving in the mouth and causing infection.

Carved handle of chew stick

A Good Tonic

Guarana plants have *caffeine* in and are made into tonic drinks in Brazil. Strong doses come in handy for getting rid of intestinal worms. Yuck!

FIGHT FOR LIGHT

Tropical plants battle with each other to reach the light that they need. Growing in the jungle can be tough, but some plants have learned to take short cuts.

GETTING A LIFT

Climbers and creepers are sneaky plants. They use other plants as their lift up to the light, often killing them in the process by strangling them or blocking out the sun. Some put out tendrils which coil around anything they come in contact with, often in a few minutes!

Another group, including ivy, haul themselves up by means of side prickles, hairs or roots.

Strong climbing plant climbs up its host

36 JUNGLE TRAIL

ANY MORE FARES, PLEASE?

Epiphytes are tree top plants which cover the branches of their host plants without harming them. They trap their own water during the heavy, tropical rains by funnelling it down to their roots.

Epiphytes on branches

FLOATING FLOWERS

Some water plants are never noticed because they spend all their time underwater. Others, such as water lilies, are obvious because they float on the surface. In some places, the leaves can completely cover the water's surface, depriving the plants below of valuable light.

Water lily

FOOD FOR ALL!

Man-eating plants are only found in science fiction stories, but there are meat-eating plants which feed on insects and small animals. Yum, yum!

MEAT-EATERS

Venus flytraps are well-known for their insect-trapping habit. Large bristles on the upper surface work like triggers. If one bristle is touched, even by a drop of water, the trap stays open, but if two or more are touched at once, the trap shuts to catch the unsuspecting victim.

Venus flytrap with supper

Pitcher plants entice insects with their bright colours and sweet smell, but once victims land on the surface, they quickly slide down to their doom.

DIY

Mistletoe is only a partial parasite. It does not completely rely on the plant it lives on as its green leaves use the sun's energy to make their own essential food. This is called *photosynthesis*.

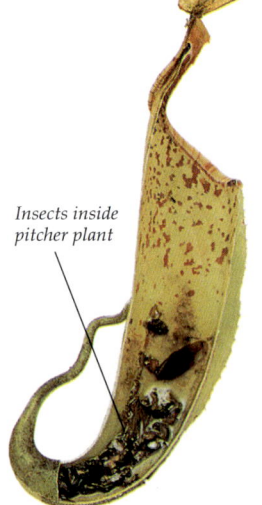

Insects inside pitcher plant

HUGE PARASITE

The world's biggest flower is a parasite called a rafflesia. Each flower can weigh up to 7 kg (15 lb) and is about 1 m (3 ft) in diameter. It has a really disgusting smell which attracts flies.

JUNGLE FOOD

Many fruits, vegetables, nuts and spices that are used nowadays in cooking come from the jungle.

Cocoa bean

Dates

Star fruit

Pineapple

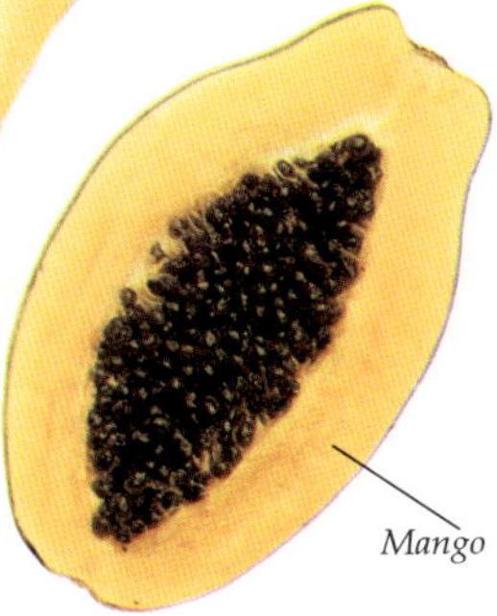

Mango

VERY PRIVATE PEOPLE

Throughout the world there are many tribes of people whose way of life has changed very little over the years. They have respect for the natural world and work with the forces of nature, rather than against them.

BELIEVE IT OR NOT...
Papua New Guinea has a population of only 4 million people, but it has over 1,000 different languages and dialects. Incredible!

THE AMAZON BASIN
The Amerindian tribes have lived in the Amazon basin for over 12,000 years. They have a vast knowledge of the plants growing in the jungle around them and use many of them everyday.

PAINTING BY SEEDS
Body painting is popular in the 143 different tribal groups in Amazonia. The people use the seeds of a plant known as *annatto* in Europe and *urucu* or *achiote* in South America. Every tribe has its own favourite patterns.

Practising the art of body painting

POISONED ARROWS

Tribal people who live in the rain forests use darts tipped with poisons to catch the animals they are after. Different tribes use different plant poisons for this job. Of course, they have to carry their arrows carefully, so they don't end up as their own victims!

Penan hunter in Borneo

...AND FINALLY!

In the Sundarbans area between India and Bangladesh, forest workers have a simple weapon against an old enemy. Tigers always attack from behind, so face masks are worn on the back of the head! Smart idea!

JUNGLE TRAIL

Home and Dry!

Rain forest people have no shortage of building materials – tree trunks for walls, palms and leaves for roofing and lianas to bind the whole lot together. Here are some of the ways that they use raw materials in and around their homes.

Thatched Roofs

In northern Thailand, the tribes people who live on the hills make houses with thatch which reaches far down on all sides, to keep the rain away from the walls. The houses are built on stilts to keep the floors dry.

The Yam House

Yams are a vital food for the tribes in New Guinea, so special buildings are erected to protect the crop. They must be well ventilated and dry, to stop the yams from going mouldy.

Chief's yam house

A Family Affair
Some tribes house the entire community in one big building while others have separate family units grouped around a clearing in the forest.

Waterside Settlements
New Guinea has such dense jungle vegetation that water travel is the easiest way to get around. Settlements are often built on the riverside, for convenience.

Essential Items
This model of a South American rain forest house shows some of the interior features you could expect to see if you went round for tea.

Sturdy tree trunks make basic frame

Hammock – a hanging bed made from cords knotted together

Fishing basket

JUNGLE TRAIL 43

TO BOLDLY GO . . .

In the 15th century, the Dutch, English and Portuguese were drawn to the forests of Southeast Asia. At the same time, in South America, the Spanish were looting the Inca and Aztec gold. But it wasn't until the 18th and 19th centuries that explorers began to develop a real scientific interest in the tropical regions.

ALEXANDER VON HUMBOLDT (1769-1859)
Von Humboldt was a German *naturalist* (a person who studies plants and animals) who had a very keen scientific interest in the natural life of the places he discovered. He explored Venezuela from 1799 onwards, and a woolly monkey from the upper Amazon is named after him!

DAVID LIVINGSTONE (1813-1873)
David Livingstone was a Scottish missionary who explored unknown territory. He mapped the course of the Zambezi River and parts of the Nile during three expeditions through the African jungle, travelling by river most of the way.

CHARLES DARWIN (1809-1882)
Best known for his theories on *evolution* (the way all creatures began and developed), Darwin joined an expedition on the ship the Beagle in 1831 to make a journal of the wildlife discovered around the South American coastline.

Henry Bates (1825-1892)

In 1848, Bates set off on an expedition to the Amazon. Over the next 11 years he collected 14,000 specimens (mostly insects) of which 8,000 were previously unknown. He kept precise notes in his endless notebooks.

Long-distance Plants

Many of the plants found in today's gardens came from far away, thanks to intrepid *botanists* (people who study plants) like John Tradescant and his son, and Joseph Pitton de Tournefort. Azaleas came from the Himalayas, tulips from Asia and fuchsias from South America.

A Future Under Threat

Every minute of every day, about 40 hectares (100 acres) of jungle are destroyed; the trees are cut down, the plants are burned and new roads are made. Modern life interrupts the old tribal ways.

Over-collecting

Beautiful, exotic jungle blooms such as orchids attract collectors, but if the collectors overdo it, the plants that they prize will become extinct.

Yellow slipper orchid

Homeless

Felling (cutting down) trees can make it difficult for some animals, such as orang-utans, to lead a normal life. Their homes and their food sources are often completely wiped out.

Orang-utan nest

Ivory Poaching

There is enormous poverty in some areas of Africa, so people are tempted to hunt elephants for their tusks, because of the huge sums of money offered by illegal ivory dealers. However, they are now more likely to end up in prison than millionaires!

Cattle Ranching

In Central and South America, the number of beef cattle rose from 1 million in 1970 to 5.5 million in 1985. The problem is that after years of grazing, the land becomes completely worn out and useless.

Index

African rain forests 14-15, 44
Amazon river 2, 10
animals 2, 3, 4, 5, 7, 10, 11, 15-27, 29, 30, 33, 46-47
apes 15, 26-27
Asian rain forests 16-17, 23, 24, 30, 44
Australasian rain forests 18-19
Aztec civilization 8

bats 29
birds 3, 5, 8, 9, 10, 14, 15, 18
buildings 42-43
butterflies 5, 13, 19, 32

canopy 3, 5
cats 30-31
Central American jungles 8-9, 25
chimpanzees 26, 27
cloud forest 4
crocodiles 33

Darwin, Charles 44

elephants 15, 20-23, 47
emergent layer 3, 4
explorers 44-45

fish 7
flowers 5, 11, 12, 14, 17, 32, 37, 39, 45, 46
food 9, 35, 39, 42
forest floor 3, 6, 17
frogs 16, 18, 29
fungi 3, 6

insects 2, 5, 9, 13, 19, 28, 29

jaguars 31

leaves 5, 12
leopards 30
lianas 5, 42
Livingstone, David 44

malaria 34
mangrove swamps 7
marsupials 19
Mayan civilization 8
monkeys 4, 11, 24-25

naturalists 44-45

panther 30
parasites 3
people 34-35, 40-41, 42-43
plants 2, 3, 4, 5, 6, 10, 11, 12, 16, 17, 32, 34, 35, 36-39, 40, 41, 42

rivers 2, 10, 44
roots 6, 12

sloth 4, 10
snakes 7, 17, 29, 32
South American rain forests 10-11, 43, 44, 45
spiders 28, 33
sugar plantations 8
swamp forests 7

Taiga 2
Tarzan 5
tigers 30
trees 2, 3, 4, 5, 6, 12, 34, 35, 46

understory 3

Acknowledgements: (KEY: t=top, b=bottom/below, c=centre, l=left, r=right)
Peter Griffith, model maker (3c), Museum of Mankind, Royal Museum of Scotland.

Picture Credits: Ardea/K Fink: 31c; Heather Angel/Biofotos: 12tl; Camera Press: 23b; Chester Zoo: 22b; Bruce Coleman Ltd/A Compost: 46b; /Luiz Claudio Marigo: 13bl; 25bl; /Rod Williams: 30tr; Colorific!/Ferorelli: 27b; Michael & Patricia Fogden: 6tr; 37t; Robert Harding Picture Library: 40tr; 40bl; 41tr; 42c; E & D Hosking: back cover tr; Hutchison Library: 20tr; /Isabella Tree: 42b; Frank Lane Picture Agency/Silvestris: 2bc; NHPA/Anthony Bannister: 47t; /Kevin Schafer: 35t; Oxford Scientific Films/Roger Brown: 6b; /P Devries: 24b; /A Plumpetre: 27t; Planet Earth Pictures/Mary Clay: front cover clb; 1c; 18c; /Peter Scoones: 12br; Ian Redmond: 21b; 26b; Silvestris: 10bl; Still Pictures/Norbert Wu: 28t; The Wildlife Collection/J Giustina: 25tr; WWF Photolibrary/Peter Jackson: 41bl.

Additional Photography: Peter Anderson, Geoff Brightling, Jane Burton, Joanna Cameron, Peter Chadwick, Geoff Dann, Philip Dowell, Frank Greenaway, Colin Keates, Dave King, Andrew McRobb, Karl Shone, Kim Taylor, Jerry Young.

Every effort has been made to trace the copyright holders. Henderson Publishing Ltd apologises for any unintentional omissions and would be pleased, in such cases, to add an acknowledgement in further editions.